THE WALKING BREAD

RICK GRAINS

TRAPEZE

This edition first published in Great Britain in 2016 by
Trapeze
an imprint of the Orion Publishing Group Ltd
Carmelite House
50 Victoria Embankment
London EC4Y 0DZ
An Hachette UK Company

10 9 8 7 6 5 4 3 2 1

A CIP catalogue record for this book is available from the British Library.

ISBN: 978 1 4091 6604 7

Printed in Italy

MIX
Paper from
responsible sources
FSC® C023419

www.orionbooks.co.uk

To Charity & Rachel

CONTENTS

CONTENTS

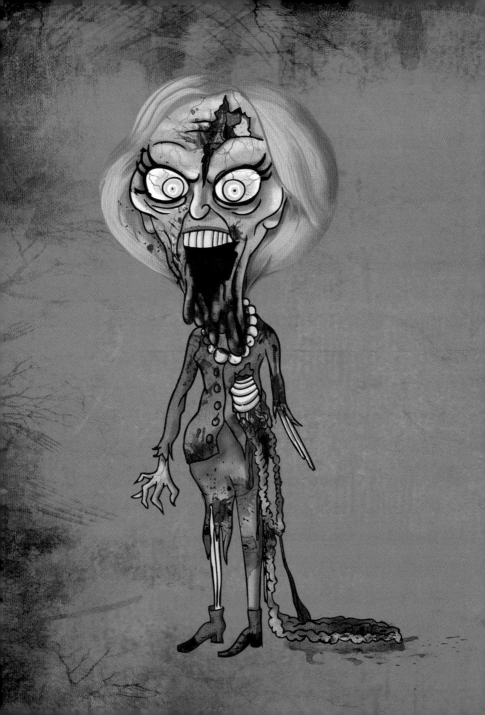

A WORD FROM
MARY BURIED

Gggggghhhhhhhaaaaaaarrrrrrrrrrrrrr!!! Soggy Bottom! Graaaaaiiiiiiiinnnnnnnsss! Ahem! Excuse me, something in my throat. Welcome to 'The Walking Bread'; a rather ghoulish collection of delectable delicacies.

When I had Paul over for dinner the other evening I was saying how there just aren't any good recipe books for the undead. (He tastes like chicken, if you're interested.) Well here we are: 22 recipes inspired by our favourite television programme. What fun! Life can get jolly boring when you're eating pedestrians all day, I can tell you, with just the odd snippet of livestock thrown in here and there, so this book couldn't come soon enough, I say!

Bone Appetit!!

MARY

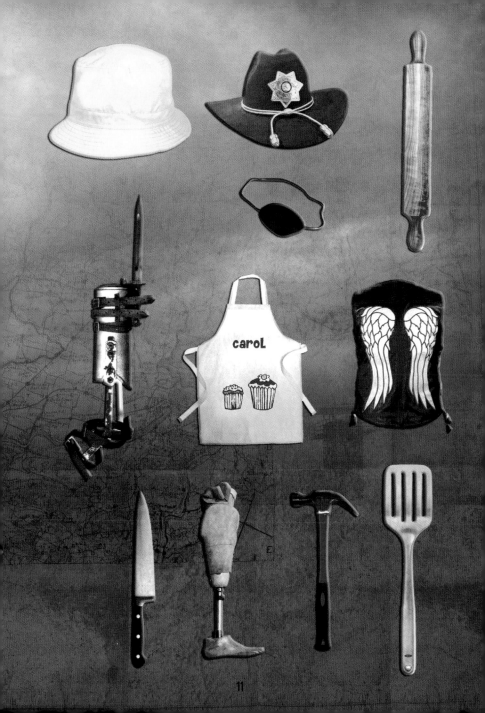

DIFFICULTY
RATING

Use the sign and choose the difficulty of your bake to survive...

HARD

'You're a survivor; you always were'

MEDIUM

'Confrontation's never been something you've had trouble with'

EASY

'Good luck, dumbass'

SEASON ONE

CARL'S CUPCAKES

Small and sweet these treats may be, but give them time and they will mature into something much stronger.

INGREDIENTS

For the cupcakes:
100g/4oz soft butter
100g/4oz caster sugar
2 medium eggs, lightly beaten (a little beating is good for you every now and then)
100g/4oz self-raising flour
1-2 tbsp/15-30ml milk

For the buttercream:
125g/5oz soft butter
250g/10oz icing sugar
1-2 tbsp (15-30ml) milk
Pink food colour

For the royal icing:
White of 1 medium egg
200-250g/10oz icing sugar
Black food colour

To decorate:
Peanut chocolate cups
Half-covered chocolate biscuit
Cola laces
Gold edible spray
Blue hard-shelled sweets

FEEDS

DIRECTIONS

Preheat the oven to 180C/165C fan assisted /350F/gas mark 4.

Clear the area of firearms. You don't want to have an accident (or two).

Line a muffin pan with paper cases.

Put all the cake ingredients except the milk into a large bowl and beat with a handheld electric mixer or wooden spoon until light and fluffy.

Add enough milk to give a dropping consistency.

Divide the mix among the paper cases.

Bake for 10-15 minutes, or until well risen (like the dead), golden brown and firm to the touch. (Make sure to keep one eye on them.) Allow to cool for a couple of minutes, then transfer the cupcakes to a wire rack to cool completely.

To make the buttercream: beat the butter in a large bowl until soft. Gently add half the icing sugar and beat until smooth.

Add the remaining icing sugar with a little milk, adding more as necessary to make a light fluffy icing.

Add the pink food colouring little by little and mix until well combined.

Spoon the icing into a piping bag fitted with a large star nozzle and pipe the pink frosting onto the cupcakes.

Add the egg whites to the icing sugar and black food colour to create the royal icing and pipe onto the cupcakes to create the hair.

Use a little royal icing to stick the peanut cup to the biscuit, wrap in the cola lace sprayed with gold. Place the hat on top of the head.

Paint eyes on the blue sweets, then press into the frosting.

Serve, enjoy and try not to think about the fact you killed your own mother.

ZOMBÉCLAIR

The best treats just keep on coming, even once you've taken a chunk out of them. One bite and you'll agree this pastry is impossible to put down.

INGREDIENTS

For the choux pastry:
65g/2 1/2 oz plain flour, sifted
Pinch of salt
50g/2oz unsalted butter, diced,
plus extra for greasing
2 medium eggs, lightly beaten

For the filling:
200ml/7fl oz double cream
5 tsp icing sugar, sifted
1 tsp vanilla extract

For the icing:
100g/3 1/2 oz milk chocolate, chopped

To decorate:
Coloured chocolate drops
Hard sweets
Purple roll-out icing
Pink frosting
Cola laces
Flaked almonds
Strawberry cream pencils

FEEDS

DIRECTIONS

Preheat the oven to 400F/200C/180C fan assisted/gas mark 6. Generously grease a baking tray with butter.

Sift the flour onto a sheet of greaseproof paper.

Put 120ml/4fl oz water, together with the salt and sugar, into a medium sized-pan and add the butter. Heat until the water is bubbling and the butter is melted, then remove from the heat and quickly tip in the flour mixture. Beat hard with a wooden spoon - don`t worry, the mixture will look messy at first but will soon come together to form a smooth, heavy dough.

Put the pan back on a low heat and beat the dough for about a minute to cook it a little - it should come away from the sides of the pan to make a smooth, glossy ball. This is much easier than attempting to shoot your undead wife with a long-range rifle, I promise.

Little by little, add the beaten egg to the dough, beating well after each addition - it may seem hard to get it to combine at first, but it will gradually come together. (This can be done in an electric mixer). The dough should be very shiny and paste-like, and fall from a spoon when lightly shaken. Spoon the pastry into a piping bag fitted with a 1.25cm/1/2in plain nozzle and pipe 6 x 10cm/4in lengths onto the greased baking tray.

Sprinkle the tray, not the pastry, with a few drops of water, and bake in the oven for 15 minutes. Then, without opening the door, reduce the oven temperature to 325F/170C/150C fan assisted/gas mark 3 and bake for 10 minutes more, or until golden brown and crisp.

Remove the tray from the oven and carefully make a small hole in the side of each eclair to allow steam to escape. Return to the oven and bake for a further 5 minutes, or until the pastry is completely crisp. Remove from the oven and transfer to a wire rack to cool.

For the filling, whip the cream with the sugar and vanilla extract in a bowl until just stiff.

Once the eclairs have cooled, cut down the length of one side of each eclair and pipe in the whipped cream.

Melt the chocolate in a microwave or over a double boiler or a bowl suspended over a pan of simmering water (do not allow the bottom of the bowl to touch the water) then allow it to cool slightly. Dip the tops of the eclairs in the chocolate and let the chocolate set before serving. Use the sweets to decorate, as pictured.

Once you've had your fill, pull out your magnum, take aim, and dispatch this sweet abomination to the after-world, where it belongs.

DARYL'S FLAPJACKETS

This is one tough cookie, but take a bite and you'll discover it's softer than you might expect.

INGREDIENTS

90ml/6 tbsp corn syrup or golden syrup
200g/8oz butter, plus extra for greasing
350g/12oz oats
A crossbow, of course
Handful of currants or raisins
Pinch of salt
300g/10oz milk chocolate
A handful of flaked almonds
Worms, if required

FEEDS

DIRECTIONS

Preheat the oven to 350F/180C/165C fan assisted/gas mark 4.

Grease a large traybake tin with oil or butter.

Place the syrup and butter in a large saucepan and heat gently until the butter has melted. Mix well with a wooden spoon.

Put the oats into a large mixing bowl and add the fruit. Add a pinch of salt then pour into the butter and syrup mixture and stir well to coat the oats. Take off the ear-necklace, it's in poor taste.

Pour the mixture into the prepared tin and spread evenly to fill the tin, making sure the surface is even.

Bake in the preheated oven for 20-25 minutes or until golden brown. Then, using a paper template as shown, cut the vest shapes with a sharp knife or craft knife while the flapjacks are still warm and soft.

Place the tin on a cooling rack and leave flapjacks in the tin until completely cold.

Meanwhile, melt the chocolate in a microwave or a bowl suspended over a pan of simmering water. (Do not allow the bottom of the bowl to touch the water.)

Put some of the melted chocolate in a piping bag fitted with a small plain nozzle and pipe along the edges of the flapjacks. Use a spoon to fill the remaining chocolate into the shape.

Before the chocolate completely cools, apply the flaked almonds in a pattern, as shown.

That's not Merle any more, so stop crying and get your knife out.

MERLE'S HANDY-SNACKS

No one likes being left behind. But when the dinner bell rings will you have the nerve to cut and run?

INGREDIENTS
500g/18oz white chocolate, in a block
135g/5oz Madeira cake or any plain cake, blitzed in a food processor
Red food colour
200g/7oz pink candy melts
Some red jam

For the handcuffs:
Jaffa chocolate cookie

You will need:
A 2in round cutter
and a fine paintbrush
Cola laces
Edible silver food spray

FEEDS

DIRECTIONS

Line a baking sheet with baking parchment. Cut 400g of the white chocolate into small pieces (setting aside a little for decoration). Place in a heatproof bowl and set over a saucepan of simmering water, (do not allow the bottom of the bowl to touch the water) stirring occasionally just until melted.

Crumble the cake into the melted chocolate, add a drop of red food colour and stir until well mixed. Use your hands to form the mixture into the shape of a hand, as pictured. Place on the lined baking sheet and leave in the fridge for about 30 minutes to firm up.

For the coating: Place the candy melts in a heatproof bowl and set over a pan of simmering water, as before, stirring occasionally just until melted.

Remove the cake hand from the fridge, then use the paintbrush to coat it with the candy coating. Then place back on the lined baking sheet.

Place somewhere cool, but not the fridge, and leave for 20-30 minutes or just until the coating has set.

Carve the remaining white chocolate into the shape of the protruding bones, as pictured, and insert into the cake hands. Dress with the jam for blood effect.

For the handcuff, use a cutter to remove the centre of the jaffa chocolate cookie. Tie together two cola laces in a pattern, as pictured, then use the edible spray to paint both silver.

As you try to stem the bleeding, comfort yourself with the thought that your severed hand will be replaced with what is essentially a very cool piece of cutlery.

LORI AND SHANE'S SECRET PASSION

Anything this forbidden has to taste scrumptious. And who cares?!
It's not like there are children involved... Oh, wait...

INGREDIENTS

For the cakes:
5 medium eggs
250g/9oz self-raising flour
250g/9oz butter or margarine (softened)
250g/9oz caster sugar
1 rounded tsp baking powder
A little milk, optional

For the buttercream:
125g/5oz soft butter
250g/10oz icing sugar
1-2 tbsp (15-30ml) milk
Pink food colour

To decorate:
4 passion fruits, seeds scooped out
4 sweet bars
Red, brown and blue food colours
Edible silver spray
Edible black food colour pen

You will need:
Heart-shaped cutter or knife

FEEDS

DIRECTIONS

Preheat oven to 350F/180C/160C fan assisted/gas mark 4. Grease a 23cm round baking tin and line the bottom with baking parchment.

Put all cake ingredients into a large mixing bowl and beat well until blended. Add a little milk as necessary to give a dropping consistency.

Spoon into the prepared tin and bake for 25-30 minutes, or until firm to the touch and a knife inserted in the centre comes out clean.

Allow to cool for a few minutes in the tin, before turning out onto a rack to cool completely. (Why not kill this time by having vigorous forest sex?)

Cut out little cakes, using a knife or heart-shaped cutter.

Cut out a large hole in the centre of each cake (being careful to keep hold of the sponge - you will need it to create a lid later).

Spoon generous amounts of passion fruit into the hole.

Trim the sponge piece you removed as necessary to make a close-fitting lid and replace on top of the passion fruit filling.

To make the buttercream: beat the butter in a large bowl until soft. Gently add half the sieved icing sugar and beat until smooth.

It didn't have to be like this.

Add the remaining icing sugar with a little milk, adding more as necessary to make a light fluffy icing.

Keeping back about a quarter of the butter icing to use later, add the pink food colouring little by little and mix until well combined.

Using a knife dipped in warm water, spread the icing over the cakes.

Divide the remaining butter icing into three and colour with red, brown and blue food colours. Pipe onto the cakes as shown, using piping bags fitted with a small, plain nozzle.

Use a pair of kitchen scissors to trim the bars to a knife shape and use the spray to colour them silver before initialling them with the black food colour pen.

Plunge the knife deep into the heart in a fit of passion, as the fruits spill forth like Shane's lifeblood and you realise this is not how you'd always pictured a threeway.

SEASON TWO

WELL WALKER TRIFLE

We've all been there: your guests are thirsty but you've got some undead in the water system. Fear not, this sweet, mushy treat will lift your spirits.

INGREDIENTS

For the sponge:
60g/2oz self-raising flour
60g/2oz butter, at room temperature
60g/2oz caster sugar
1 egg
1/4 tsp baking powder

For the trifle:
A 'well'-shaped receptacle, gingerbread man cutter
2 packets green jelly
300ml/1/2 pint custard
Red and black food colour
Cola laces
A length of rope, a sturdy pipe, Glenn
Gummy teeth, chocolate drops and frosting, to decorate

FEEDS

DIRECTIONS

Check the pipe. Always check the pipe.

Prepare the jelly as directed on the packets. (Don't put it in the fridge, as you need it to remain liquid.)

Preheat the oven to 350F/180C/160C fan assisted/gas mark 4.

Place the ingredients for the sponge cake into a large bowl and mix together with a handheld electric mixer.

Pour two-thirds of the mixture into 2 non-stick 7 in/18cm round cake tins.

Pour the rest of the mixture into the gingerbread cutter.

Place both in the oven for 15-25 minutes until golden brown.

Cool on a wire rack.

Remember, all's well that ends well.

Once cooled, cut a circle of the sponge the size of the receptacle to form the base of the trifle. Push into the bottom of the receptacle and pour the custard on top.

Use the sweets, chocolate drops, frosting and food colouring to decorate the face of the gingerbread man as shown.

Before the jelly has completely set, insert your walker and affix a cola lace around it under the arms.

Keep pulling and pulling until it's time to split.

DALE'S TEAR N SHARE

Love will tear us apart... that or a marauding zombie hiding behind a cow. Who knows in this cruel world? All you can do is get stuck into this tasty tragedy.

INGREDIENTS

You will need:
A strong moral compass
and a weak dress sense

For the brioche body:
250g/9oz plain flour
100g/4oz butter
2 rounded tbsp caster sugar
Pinch of salt
7g sachet fast-action yeast
3 eggs, lightly beaten
Egg yolk, to glaze
2-3 sugar cubes, lightly crushed

To decorate:
Strawberry laces
Strawberry or raspberry jam
3 madeleines
Piped royal icing
Yellow and green roll-out icing
Red and black food colour
(No cutlery is required when eating this dish)

FEEDS

DIRECTIONS

To make the brioche: tip the flour into a food processor fitted with a plastic kneading blade and add the butter. Process until the mixture looks like breadcrumbs. Stir in the caster sugar, a good pinch of salt and the yeast.

Add the eggs and mix to a soft dough, then knead in the machine for 2 minutes.

Butter a brioche mould or 2-pint loaf tin. Sprinkle a layer of flour onto a work surface and tip the dough onto it. With floured hands, knead very briefly to form a ball, then drop the dough into the tin, smooth side up. Cover with cling film and leave to rise in a warm place, until doubled in size, about 2 hrs.

Try not to be distracted by any stricken livestock.

Preheat the oven to 400F/ 200C/ 180C fan assisted/ gas mark 6. Brush the top of the brioche with egg yolk, then sprinkle over crushed sugar and bake for 20-25 minutes, until golden brown and the loaf sounds hollow when tapped. Tip out onto a wire rack and leave to cool.

Use a knife to make an incision along the underside of the brioche and remove some of the filling, then insert the strawberry laces and jam to create the innards. Patch up the hole using the removed brioche and some royal icing to seal.

To decorate, trim 2 madeleines to use for arms, and the remaining madeleine for the head. attach to the body with icing, and leave to set hard. Use the roll-out icing to create the hat and shirt.

Pipe on the royal icing for the beard and eyes, adding black and red food colour to create the mouth and pupils.

There's no way to enjoy this one without making a mess. Just try not to rip your Hawaiian shirt.

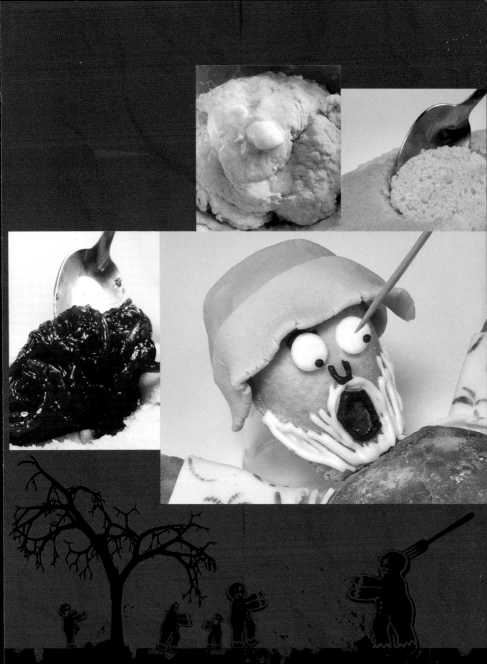

JUST LOOK AT THE FLOUR LIZZIE

SOPHIA'S BARNSTORMING BANQUET

The dish we've all been searching for – for such a long time. It may be unappetising to some but it's sure to end your party with a bang.

INGREDIENTS

A barn full of walkers
2 packets of toaster tarts
A small quantity of royal icing
1 packet milk chocolate malted biscuits
1 packet fizzy strawberry laces
1 packet chocolate sticks
1 packet raisin biscuits
1 packet Jelly men sweets
Red food colour
5ml/0.2 fl oz water

FEEDS

DIRECTIONS

Use the toaster tarts to make the four walls of the barn and stick them together using royal icing.

Use the royal icing throughout the construction to fix all the parts together.

Use a knife to shape the upper walls to fit the roof.

Once the toaster tarts have been laid onto the roof, use the malted biscuits and then the strawberry straws to make the thatching.

Decorate the front of the barn with chocolate sticks, using a knife to cut them to length (remembering to leave space for the windows) and affixing them to the toaster tarts with royal icing.

Cut raisin biscuits to form the doors of the barn. Then cut a small hole in each and insert a strawberry lace between them to create the chain lock.

Use the jelly men sweets to decorate and add the food colour and a little water for blood-splatter effect.

Now open the doors, ready your weapons and take aim; it's tea time!

MICHONNE'S PET FOOD

'Have you ever been covered in so much jam that you didn't know if it was yours, or walkers', or your friends? Huh? Then you don't KNOW!'

INGREDIENTS

200g/7oz plain flour, plus extra to dust
1 1/2 tsp/7g dried yeast
1/2 tsp salt
15g/1/2oz caster sugar
25g/1oz butter, cut into small pieces
75ml/3fl oz warm milk
50ml/2fl oz warm water
1 medium egg, lightly beaten
Vegetable or sunflower oil, to deep-fry
30ml/6tsp strawberry jam
1 packet liquorice laces
Some yellow hard sweets
A small amount of edible glue
750g/26oz milk chocolate
250g/10oz brown ready-to-roll icing

For the glaze:
250g/9oz icing sugar
3 1/2 tbsp/21ml whole milk
2 1/2 tsp/18ml vanilla extract

You will need:
A gingerbread cutter
A sharp knife or, better,
a katana

FEEDS

DIRECTIONS

Don't let others help with this one, you're better off working on your own.

Combine the flour, yeast, salt and sugar in a large bowl and mix well. Put the butter into a second small bowl with the warm milk and water, and stir to melt. Pour this into the mixing bowl, along with the egg, and stir until it comes together into a dough: it should be firm, but soft.

Turn out onto a lightly floured surface and knead until smooth and elastic (about 10 minutes). Put into a lightly greased bowl, cover with cling film and leave to prove in a warm place for about an hour.

Turn out the dough again onto a lightly floured surface and knead lightly. Roll out, using your hands as well as the rolling pin to encourage the dough into a flat shape.

Dipping the cutter in flour between shapes to stop it sticking, cut out 2-3 doughnut men, re-rolling the dough as necessary in between each one. Cover and allow to rise again in a warm place for half an hour or so.

Prepare the glaze by sifting the icing sugar into a medium bowl. Slowly stir in the milk and vanilla extract until the mixture is smooth, adding a little extra milk if necessary. Cover the glaze with cling film and set aside.

Heat up the oil in a deep-fat fryer to 320F/160C. Carefully fry the men one at a time for a few minutes each side, turning once they are golden. Remove and allow to drain on kitchen paper for a minute or two.

Cut off both arms and push the knife into the holes. Then use the knife to create a hole around the mouth, as shown. (It is essential that both the teeth and arms are removed, to avoid potential infection.) Fill a piping bag fitted with small nozzle with strawberry jam and squeeze jam into each hole, as shown.

Use a small amount of jam to affix the sweetie eyes.

Using the edible glue, create liquorice nooses to go around the men's necks. (You don't want these guys getting away from you.)

For the dipping sauce, melt the chocolate in a bowl over a pan of simmering water and pour into an empty jar. Roll out the icing, using flour on the surface and rolling pin, and shape into a hood over the jar.

Once complete, take your new pets for a walk. As with normal pets, just play with them until you get bored (and then eat them).

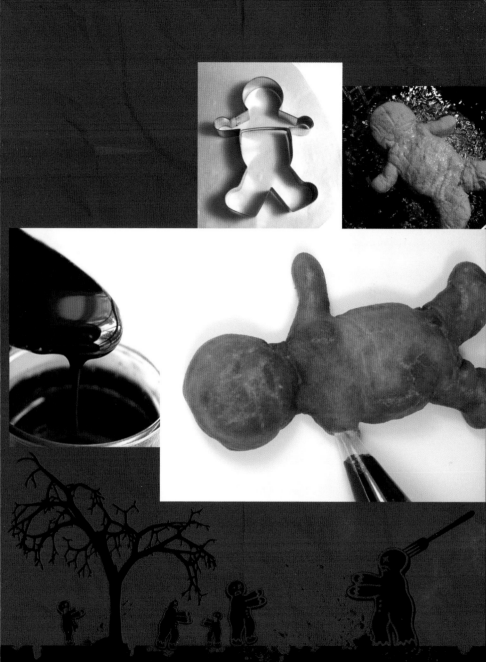

SEASON THREE

VICTIM JELLY JARS

Some people might think it's weird to keep a secret collection of decapitated cake-pop heads. Don't invite those people to this party.

INGREDIENTS

175g/6oz white or milk chocolate, in drops or broken into pieces

350g/12oz Madeira cake or any basic sponge cakes, chocolate or plain, blitzed in a food processor

2 packets of green jelly

400g/14oz white chocolate, in drops or chopped into pieces

100g/4oz milk chocolate (for decorating)

A few drops of pink food colouring, optional

Cola laces and chocolate sprinkles, to decorate

Cake pop sticks

Edible glue

Black food colouring

You will need:

4 small jars (ideally of equal size and shape) - we used 4 condiment jars and boiled the labels off them

Cocktail sticks

FEEDS

DIRECTIONS

Line a baking sheet with baking parchment. Place 175g of chocolate in a heatproof bowl and set over a saucepan of simmering water (do not let the bottom of the bowl touch the water), stirring occasionally just until melted.

Crumble the cake into the melted chocolate and stir until well mixed. Use your hands to roll the mixture into balls each about as large as a golf ball. Insert a cake pop stick into each ball, place on the lined baking sheet and leave in the fridge for about 30 minutes to firm up.

Meanwhile, prepare the jelly and pour the mixture halfway up the jars.

For the white chocolate coating: place 400g of white chocolate in a heatproof bowl and set over a pan of simmering water, stirring occasionally just until melted. Remove from the heat and stir in the food colouring. (if you'd like to colour the white chocolate).

Remove the cake pops from the fridge, then dip each one into the chocolate coating and either insert upright into the polystyrene block or place back on the lined baking sheet.

Place somewhere cool, but not the fridge, and leave for 20-30 minutes or just until the chocolate has set. Before the coating sets on the cake pops, you can roll them in sprinkles.

Melt the milk chocolate over a warm bath of water. Decorate your cake pops' faces using the chocolate and a piping bag, before removing the sticks.

Once the cake pops and jelly are both set, place the cake pops in the jar and fill them up with jelly. Use a toothpick to pierce the top of each and, making a hole in the lid of the jar, insert the toothpick up through the lid to hold the cake pop in place.

Leave to set and, when ready, remove the toothpick.

Now lock the door and go back to terrorising the community of survivors of which you have appointed yourself leader.

GLENN AND MAGGIE'S
FINGER FOOD

Love can take root in the unlikeliest of places and can be as hard to kill as a walker. Will you say 'I do' to this most heartwarming of dishes?

INGREDIENTS
1 packet sponge fingers
200g/7oz white chocolate
Some flaked almonds
Cocoa powder, for dusting
Green and red food colour
Assorted sweets, to construct the ring
Edible glue

You will need:
Hershel's blessing

FEEDS

DIRECTIONS

You may want to cut down the sponge fingers with a sharp knife to get them to the appropriate length.

Warm the chocolate over a bath of water until it is ready to spread. Using a knife, cover the sponge fingers.

Take a piece of flaked almond and apply to the tip to create the fingernail.

Use a toothpick to draw creases in the chocolate.

Mix the food colours with a small amount of water and then use the brush to apply first the green to colour the finger and then red to the base of the ring finger.

Use a brush to add the cocoa powder, creating an ageing effect.

Finally, create the 'ring' using sweets and edible glue and attach it to the finger.

Go forward in the knowledge that one or both of you is likely to turn into a lifeless bloodsucking monster... but hey, that's marriage.

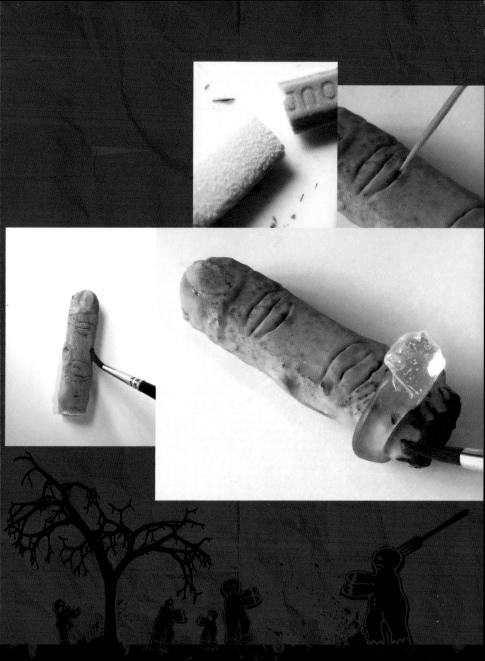

JUDITH'S SHORTBREAD SNACKS

Looking for some light relief from the unrelenting horror of the undead apocalypse? Against all odds, these sweet treats offer a glimmer of hope at even the bleakest of parties.

INGREDIENTS
100g/4oz spreadable butter
50g/2oz caster sugar
150g/5oz plain flour
25g/1oz cornflour

To decorate:
White of 1 medium egg
500g/1lb icing sugar, sifted
Black food colour

You will need:
A knife
An edible black pen

FEEDS

DIRECTIONS

Preheat the oven to 325F/165C/150C fan assisted/gas mark 3.

Line a large baking tray with non-stick baking parchment.

Cream the butter and sugar together in a mixing bowl with a wooden spoon until creamy (i.e. baby soft).

Mix together the flour and cornflour and add it to the butter/sugar, encouraging it to blend in with the back of the spoon.

Turn the lumpy mix out onto a work surface or silicon sheet dusted with flour, and work the dough gently with your hands until it comes together - don't overdo it or the dough will become oily and tough (the wrong kind of tough, that is).

Wrap and chill for at least an hour.

Dust the work surface and a rolling pin well with flour and roll out the dough very gently, pushing it together with your hands as cracks form.

Cut shapes with the knife. This isn't easy but it's simpler than an emergency caesarean.

Put the egg white in a bowl and whisk lightly with a fork. Add the icing sugar little by little, beating with a wooden spoon until the texture is of a piping consistency. Divide into three.

Attach a plain writing nozzle to a small piping bag and fill with white piping icing and pipe on the outline of the baby suit.

Allow to dry. Add a few drops of water to the icing to give a runny consistency and carefully spoon into the outline of the shirt, teasing it into the corners with a small brush. Allow to dry.

Use the pen to write the pattern shown.

Once created, it's time to christen the dish. Avoid the temptation to use names of any recently deceased members of your group.

THE GOVERNOR'S EYE POPS

Governors, lock up your daughters. Michonne's in town and she's about to serve just desserts.

INGREDIENTS

For the eyeballs:
350g/12oz Madeira cake or any basic sponge cakes
400g/14oz white chocolate, in drops or chopped into pieces
200g/7oz white candy melts

For the sugar glass:
18ml/1/2 cup water
177ml/3/4 cup light corn syrup
350g/14oz granulated sugar
10ml/2 tsp peppermint extract
Food colours, to decorate

You will need:
Sugar thermometer
Fine paint brush (as well as an undead daughter whom you have hiden from the world)

FEEDS

DIRECTIONS

Line a baking sheet with baking parchment. Place the chocolate in a heatproof bowl and set over a saucepan of simmering water, stirring occasionally just until melted.

Grate the cake into the melted chocolate and stir until well mixed. Use your hands to roll the mixture into balls each about as large as an eyeball. Place on the lined baking sheet and leave in the fridge for about 30 minutes to firm up.

For the coating: Place the candy melts in a heatproof bowl and set over a pan of simmering water, stirring occasionally just until melted.

Remove the cake pops from the fridge, then, using a fork, dip each one into the coating and place back on the lined baking sheet.

Place somewhere cool, but not the fridge, and leave for 20-30 minutes or just until the coating has set.

Once set, use a paintbrush to apply the food colour to create the details of the eye.

For the sugar glass: line a baking tray with foil, or use a heatproof glass tray. Spray with non-stick baking spray.

In a medium saucepan, combine the sugar, water and corn syrup. Stir the mixture over medium heat until the sugar dissolves, then turn up the heat to bring to a boil. Stop stirring, and insert the thermometer, wetting the sides of the pan with a damp pastry brush as necessary to prevent crystals forming.

Cook the mixture until the temperature reaches 285F/140C. Immediately remove the pan from the heat and take out the thermometer. Let the mixture stand until all the bubbles have stopped forming on the surface.

Add a few drops of peppermint flavouring.

Quickly pour the mixture onto the baking tray, lifting the tray from side to side to spread the mix. Don't worry if it's not perfectly smooth or has holes in it. Let the candy cool to room temperature.

Once the candy has cooled, use the handle of a knife to break it up.

Jam the glass shards into the cake pops, flick with red colour, and don't be squeamish: remember, this is a survival situation.

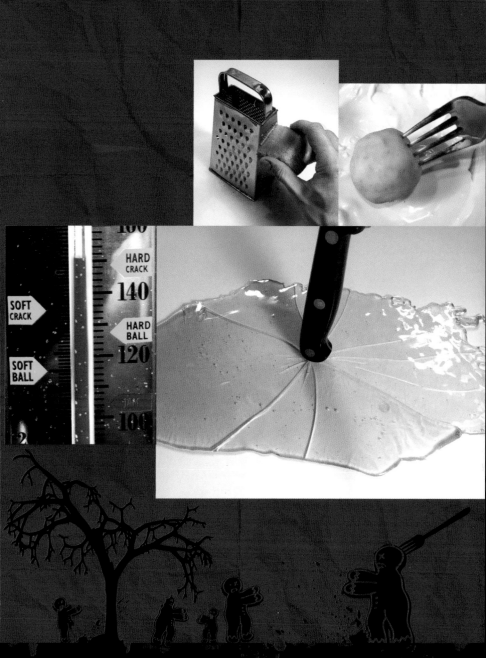

SEASON FOUR

HERSHEL'S DECAP DELIGHTS

An oldie but a goodie, this dish brings out the best in people.

INGREDIENTS
15g/1/2oz butter
100g/4oz mini marshmallows
175g/6oz krispy cereal
400g/14oz white chocolate, in drops or
chopped into pieces
Pink food colour

You will need:
A cocktail stick
Tin foil
Some green hard-shelled sweets
Food colours, to decorate
Have a large knife nearby in case of any
emergency amputations

FEEDS

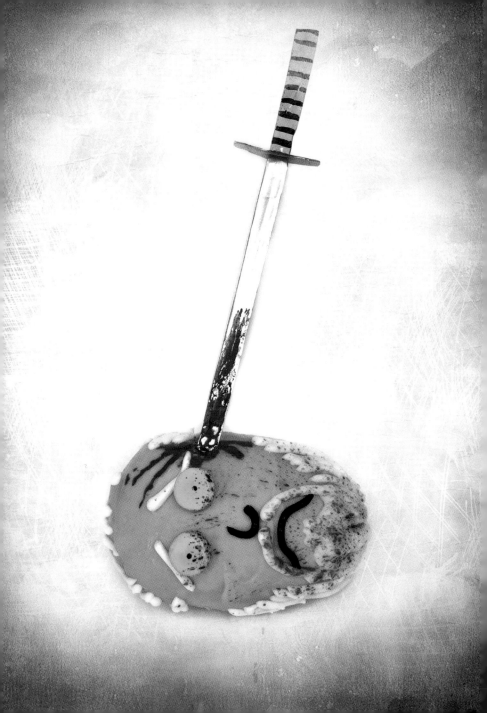

DIRECTIONS

Grease a 32 x 23cm / 13 x 9 inch traybake tin.

Melt the butter in a large, heavy-based saucepan over low heat.

Add the marshmallows and cook gently until they are completely melted and blended, stirring constantly. Mix well.

Take the pan off the heat and immediately add the cereal, mixing lightly until well coated.

Let the mix cool before shaping into heads.

For the chocolate coating: Place the chocolate (or candy melts) in a heatproof bowl and set over a pan of simmering water, stirring occasionally just until melted. Add a little food colour to the white chocolate to turn it pink.

Remove the cake pops from the fridge, then dip each one into the chocolate coating and place back on the lined baking sheet.

Press the hard-shelled sweets into the heads for eyes and decorate with a little black food colour.

Place somewhere cool, but not the fridge, and leave for 20-30 minutes or just until the chocolate has set.

Use the piping icing and food colour to decorate.

Wrap the cocktail stick in a small piece of folded silver foil, and decorate with food colour to create the handle. Pierce one side of the cake pop.

As you await the swing of the knife, think of your family.

CAROL'S TOUGH COOKIES

This recipe is a walk in the park (well, a walk in the woods to be exact). It might not end well for your guests but once you've done it you'll feel like a new person.

INGREDIENTS
280g/10oz plain flour
200g/7oz firm butter
100g/4oz icing sugar
2 egg yolks
1 tsp vanilla extract/essence

To decorate:
100g/4oz icing sugar
1 egg white
Yellow colouring
1 pack yellow chocolate drops
Red food colour
Flower-shaped cutter

FEEDS

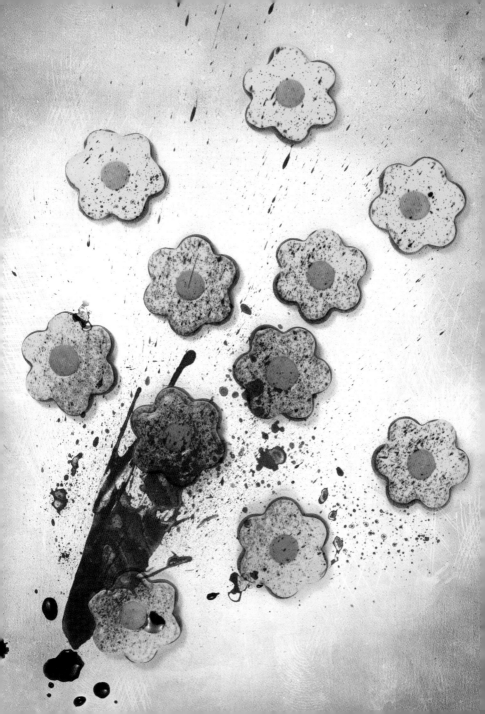

DIRECTIONS

Put the flour in a bowl. Cut the butter into small pieces and add to the flour.

Look at the pretty flowers...

Rub the butter into the flour with your fingertips until the mix looks like breadcrumbs.

Add the icing sugar, egg yolks and vanilla extract or essence and mix to a dough.

Put into a plastic bag and chill for at least 30 minutes.

Keep looking at the pretty flowers...

Roll out the cookie dough on a lightly floured surface to about 5mm thickness.

Cut out shapes with a 'flower-shaped' cutter and place them on a baking tray lined with baking parchment. Put back into the fridge to chill again for 30 minutes.

Meanwhile, preheat the oven to 350F/180C/160C fan assisted/gas mark 4.

JUST LOOK AT THE GODDAMN FLOWERS OKAY?!

Bake the cookies for 12-15 minutes, until the cookies are beginning to brown around the edges.

Remove from the oven and allow to cool on the tray before carefully lifting off.

For the royal icing, sift the icing sugar into a small bowl and add the egg white, little by little, until a piping consistency is achieved. Add the yellow food colour. Place some of the icing in a bag with a plain nozzle and pipe the outline of each flower.

Add more egg white to the remaining icing mix until a flooding consistency is reached.

Flood the tops of the cookies with the yellow icing. Allow to partially set before adding the yellow chocolate drop.

Decorate liberally with a splatter of red food colour as you feel your humanity ebb away.

TERMINUS TREATS

Now that you've reached the end of the road, you have to choose: you're either the baker or you're the doughnut.

INGREDIENTS

For the track and sign:
Flaked chocolate bars
Chocolate biscuit bars
A little melted chocolate
Malted milk biscuits
Chocolate sticks
As much human flesh as
you can eat

For the edible soil:
70g/2 1/2oz plain cooking
chocolate, chopped into pieces
100g/4oz caster sugar
2 tbsp water

For the fires:
Chocolate Swiss roll
Hard-shelled chocolate sweets

For the buttercream:
125g/5oz soft butter
250g/10oz icing sugar
1-2 tbsp (15-30ml) milk
Red and yellow food colours

You will need:
A star-shaped nozzle

FEEDS

DIRECTIONS

For the chocolate soil: heat the sugar and water in a pan and insert a sugar thermometer.

When the sugar reaches 266F/130C, take off the heat.

If you haven't got a thermometer, wait until all the sugar is dissolved and starting to change to a medium-brown colour.

Add the chocolate bits and stir with a whisk. Make sure all the sugar coats the chocolate and stir for about 2 minutes.

Empty out the mixture on to a piece of foil to cool, and steer clear of the trough if you want to save your neck.

Arrange the flaked chocolate bars in a 'v' shape on a board to give the sense of perspective, and dress with the crumbled chocolate soil.

Cut the chocolate biscuit bars and use a little melted chocolate to reattach them so they are the correct size to fit the track.

Stick the malted milk biscuits together with melted chocolate as shown.

Wait to set hard and attach the chocolate sticks with more melted chocolate to create the TERMINUS sign.

Cut the Swiss roll into slices and add hard sweets and sticks held down with melted chocolate.

Make the buttercream and split into two. Colour one half red and the other yellow and spoon into a piping bag with a 3mm/1/2in star-shaped nozzle. Pipe onto the twigs to create the fire effect.

Wait for Carol to blow the joint before leaving this sweet hell hole behind...

TREE WALKER CRUDITÉS

Get back to nature with this unforgettable snack attack...
And you thought vegetables were good for you.

INGREDIENTS

For the flatbread:
400g/14oz rye flour
1 tsp fine sea salt
10g/1/3oz fresh yeast
350ml/1/2 pint water

To decorate:
1 cucumber, sliced
Some carrots, cut into sticks
Some celery stalks
1 red pepper
A dip of your choice (preferably white in colour)
A few pine nuts
1 tomato
1 radish
1 pickled beetroot and 2 olives
A handful of parsley and chives

FEEDS

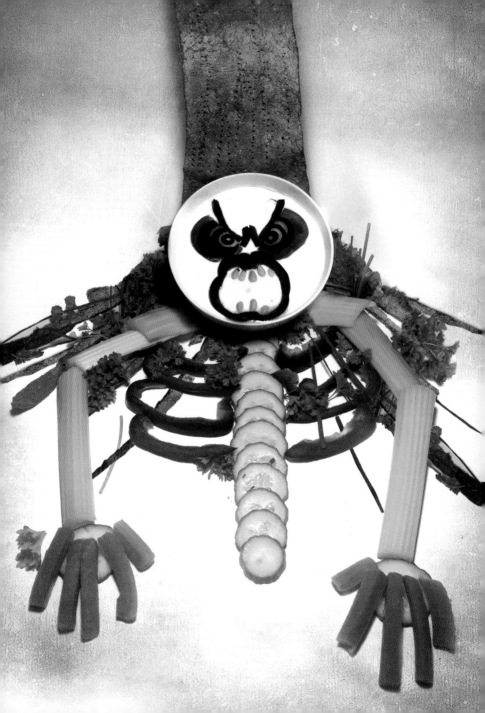

DIRECTIONS

Get in touch with your roots.

Put the flour into a large bowl and add the salt. Warm the water to about 71F/22C. Crumble the yeast into the water and whisk until the water is milky and the yeast has virtually dissolved.

Pour the yeast mixture into the flour and stir until it comes together into a dough. Cover the bowl with a cloth and leave in a warm place for an hour. Line a baking sheet with baking parchment. Preheat the oven to 400F/200C/180C fan assisted/gas mark 6.

Roll out the dough into a rectangle roughly 30cm in size.

Pierce the surface of the dough all over with holes, using a fork or skewer. Bake for 15-18 minutes until the bread is truly crisp.

Using a knife, cut a large section of the bread to create the tree trunk and then cut smaller sections to create the roots.

To decorate the walker, use slices of cucumber to form the spine and palms; carrot sticks to form the fingers; celery stalks to create the arms and shoulders. Slice up a red pepper to form the rib cage.

Promise yourself you'll never eat organic again.

Pour out a bowl of dip and use the pepper to form eyebrows and mouth and use pine nuts for teeth. The eyes are formed out of slices of tomatoes, radishes, beetroots and olives.

Decorate the whole thing liberally with herbs to create the surrounding vegetation.

Instruct your guests to stand back and let nature take its hideous course.

SEASON FIVE

BOB'S TAINTED MEAT TREATS

This Zom-BBQ offers a fantastic meaty treat, but be warned - it can leave you with a very bitter aftertaste...

INGREDIENTS
230ml/8fl oz ketchup
3 tbsp brown sugar
2 tbsp soy sauce
6 individual spare ribs (ask your
butcher if they have any tainted meat)
1 pack of small bread rolls
Some parsley stalks

FEEDS

DIRECTIONS

Place the spare ribs in a large, flat roasting dish. Mix the ketchup, sugar and soy sauce together and brush the mixture all over the ribs, keeping back a little for basting later.

Preheat the oven to 300F/150C/130C fan assisted/gas mark 2. Roast the ribs in the centre of the oven for 1 1/2 - 2 hours. Halfway through

cooking, cover the ribs with tin foil to protect them from drying out.

About 30 minutes before the end of cooking, brush the ribs with the remaining sauce, re-cover and finish cooking.

Let them rest, covered, for about 10 minutes.

Remember, it's not cannibalism if you use a dipping sauce.

Use a knife to cut holes in the bread rolls and use the off-cuts to create tongues for the boots.

The boot laces are created by perforating the bread with a knife and inserting parsley stalks.

Insert the ribs into the shoes, carefully using toothpicks to keep them upright if necessary.

Let your cries of horror slowly turn to a blood-curdling cackle as your guests realise just what it is that you've served them.

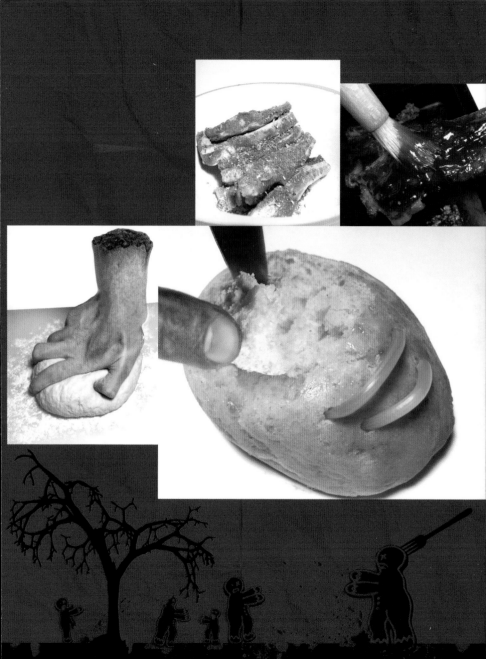

BITE THE BREAD,
FEAR THE FILLING.

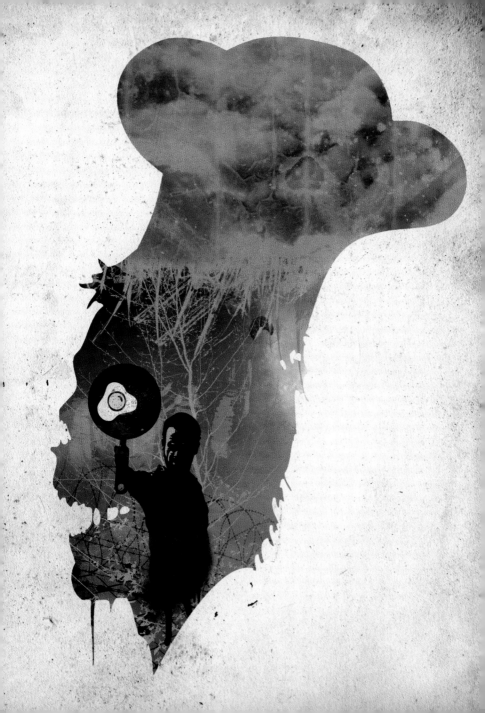

BITER BRAINS BITES

There are so many ways to take down a walker, each of them more delicious than the last. Let your guests embrace their violent side with these delicious head candies...

INGREDIENTS

For the cupcakes:
100g/4oz soft butter
100g/4oz caster sugar
2 medium eggs, lightly beaten
100g/4oz self-raising flour
Gel food colour
1-2 tbsp/15-30ml milk
100g/4oz strawberry jam

For the buttercream:
125g/5oz soft butter
250g/10oz icing sugar
1-2 tbsp/15-30ml milk
Pink food colour

To decorate:
Chocolate sticks
Fizzy sweets
Edible glue or melted chocolate
Sweet bar
Black and silver edible food spray
Red food color

FEEDS

DIRECTIONS

Preheat the oven to 350F/180C/160C fan assisted/gas mark 4.

Line a 12-hole muffin pan with paper muffin cases.

Put all the cake ingredients except the colour, milk and jam into a large bowl and beat with a handheld electric mixer or wooden spoon until light and fluffy.

Add enough milk to give a 'dropping' consistency.

Divide the mix between the paper cases, holding back about half for covering.

Make a small well in each mix, and add a tablespoon of the jam. Cover each with the remaining mix.

Bake for 10-15 minutes, or until well risen, golden brown and firm to the touch. Allow to cool for a couple of minutes, then transfer the cupcakes to a wire rack to cool completely.

To make the buttercream: beat the butter in a large bowl until soft. Gently add half the icing sugar and beat until smooth.

Add the remaining icing sugar with a little milk, adding more as necessary to make a light fluffy icing.

Add the pink food colouring little by little and mix until well combined.

Spread about a third of the butter icing over the cupcakes, then spoon the remaining icing into a piping bag fitted with a large, plain nozzle and pipe cranial swirls on top of each cake.

The arrow is created using a chocolate stick and fizzy sweets, held together with a little edible glue (or melted chocolate).

The knife is created using the sweet bar, sprayed black and silver (with a chocolate drop for the rivet).

With a paintbrush, apply the black and red food colour to create the entry wounds.

Remember, nothing less than a head shot will do, so aim well.

SEASON SIX

RICK'S TRANSFORMATIONAL TREATS

Arguably the most popular dish in the series, this cookie will nonetheless do what it takes to survive, going from wholesome goodness to something that will suit much darker tastes.

INGREDIENTS
500g/18oz plain flour
400g/14oz firm butter
200g/7oz icing sugar
Yolks of 4 medium eggs
2 tsp vanilla extract/essence
A Colt Magnum

To decorate:
200g/7oz icing sugar
Whites of 2 medium eggs
Brown, black and red food colours
Yellow sugar stars

You will need:
A gingerbread man cutter
An increasingly loose moral code

FEEDS

DIRECTIONS

Wake up, you've missed a lot already...
Now get up and go to war.

Put the flour in a bowl. Cut the butter into
small pieces and add to the flour.

Rub the butter into the flour with
your fingertips until the mix looks like
breadcrumbs.

Add the sugar, egg yolks and vanilla extract
or essence and mix to form a dough.

Put into a plastic bag and chill for at least
30 minutes.

Roll out the cookie dough on a lightly floured
surface to about 5mm/1/4 in thickness.

Cut out shapes with a 'gingerbread man'
cutter and place them on a baking tray
lined with baking parchment. Make sure to
use a knife to cut a hat shape into the
head of one of the cookies. Put back into the
fridge to chill again for 30 minutes.

When using the knife, remember not to kill
the living.

Meanwhile, preheat the oven to
350F/180C/160C fan assisted/ gas mark 4.

Bake for 12-15 minutes, until the cookies
are beginning to brown around the edges
(they will be soft, but will harden as they
cool).

OK, you can kill the living, but only if they're
trying to kill you.

Remove from the oven and allow to cool on
the tray before carefully lifting off.

Sift the icing sugar into a small bowl and
add egg white, little by little, beating well
until a piping consistency is reached. Divide
into thirds and colour one third brown
and one third black, leaving the remaining
third white. With a piping bag fitted with
a small plain nozzle (or small paper piping
bag with the end cut off), pipe the outline
of the jackets, shirts, faces and hairs on the
individual cookies with the coloured icings,
making a little grey with black and white
icing for the beard. Loosen the texture of the
brown, black and white icings with a little
water, then carefully fill the jacket shapes
using a small teaspoon. Apply yellow stars to
one of the cookies. Allow to set.

Splatter season 6 Rick in red food colour.

Actually, thinking about it, just kill anyone.
It's fine.

est 2003
GEORGIA
TERMINUS
B-B-Q
& Grill
all our meats are flesh!
WE'D LOVE TO
HAVE YOU FOR DINNER

GINGER DEAD HERD

Mmmmmm... Graaaaaiiinnnnnsss! It's dinner time! The only question now is who is doing the eating: you or them?!

INGREDIENTS

700g / 1lb 9oz plain flour
4 tsp baking powder
4 tsp ground ginger (or more to taste)
200g / 7oz cold butter
300g / 12oz light brown soft sugar
6 tbsp golden syrup
2 medium eggs, lightly beaten
A little flour for dusting

You will need:
A gingerbread man cutter
(ideally several cutters of
different sizes)

To decorate:

Whites of 2 medium eggs
1kg / 2lb icing sugar, sifted
Red and black food paste colours
Hard-shelled sweets
Gummy teeth (take care not to get bitten
during preparation)

FEEDS

DIRECTIONS

Preheat the oven to 400F/200C/180C fan assisted/gas mark 6. Grease two baking trays or line with non-stick baking parchment.

You'll need to move quickly; these walkers may be slow but before you know it there's a whole herd upon you.

Put the flour, baking powder and ginger into a bowl and mix well. Cut the butter into the flour mixture in small pieces and rub in with your fingers until it resembles breadcrumbs.

Add the sugar, syrup and eggs and mix to form a dough. Put into a plastic bag and chill for half an hour. (You won't be able to chill but at least try to stay calm.)

Roll out the dough on a surface lightly dusted with flour. Cut out gingerbread men with the cutter and place them on the tray. Bake for 10-12 minutes or until beginning to brown around the edges. Transfer to a rack to cool and harden.

Put the egg whites in a bowl and whisk lightly with a fork. Add the icing sugar little by little, beating with a wooden spoon until the texture is of a piping consistency. (Wooden spoon, fork, socket wrench, whatever you have to hand. They're coming, for God's sake!)

Use a small amount of the icing to fix the hard sweet eyes and gummy teeth to the gingerbread men. Colour a tiny portion of icing black. Colour the remaining icing red and spoon it into a piping bag fitted with a small, plain writing nozzle and pipe on the blood details. Add eye details with the black icing.

Now you're ready! In a worst-case scenario you may need to cover yourself in bits of gingerbread dough and stuff your pockets with gummy sweets to avoid detection.

THE
BREAD WILL
RISE

LUCILLE (KRISPY KILLER)

A real home run of a dish. You may have to wait a while, though, to see how this one turns out...

INGREDIENTS
50g/2oz butter
300g/12oz mini marshmallows
175g/6oz krispy cereal
175g/6oz milk chocolate and 100g/4oz of dark chocolate, in drops or broken into pieces
Cola laces
Silver edible food spray
Red food colour

You will need:
A pastry brush
A palette knife
To know at least one nursery rhyme

FEEDS

DIRECTIONS

Grease a 32 x 23cm / 13 x 9 inch traybake tin.

Melt the butter in a large, heavy-based saucepan over low heat. When choosing a saucepan, line them up on your kitchen counter and point to them in sequence saying 'eeny meeny miny mo' under your breath.

Add the marshmallows and cook gently until they are completely melted and blended, stirring constantly. Mix well.

Take the pan off the heat and immediately add the cereal, mixing lightly until well coated.

Let the mix cool before shaping into a bat. It will be very sticky, so wet hands if necessary.

For the chocolate coating: place the milk and dark chocolates in separate heatproof bowls and set over a pan of simmering water, stirring occasionally just until melted. Remove from the heat and use a palette knife to apply to the exterior of the bat: first the milk chocolate and then brush the darker chocolate on top to create streaks and decoration.

Tie the sugar laces into a 'barbed wire' pattern, spray with edible silver and allow to dry before tying around the bat.

Add the red food colour to a small amount of water and use a brush to flick spray onto the bat until it looks suitably gory.

Try not to be disappointed with this dish. I know we've all been waiting a long time but we're just going to have to wait a little longer, okay?

ENJOYED THIS?
COMPLETE THE TRILOGY!

Great recipes. No meth-in around.

Ba king Ba d

99.1% PURE 100% EDIBLE

WALTER WHEAT

Edible recipes from the Seven Kingdoms

GAME OF SCONES

ALL MEN MUST DINE

JAMMY LANNISTER

SHARE YOUR RECIPE PICS USING

#WalkingBread

AUTHOR'S NOTE

This book is a tribute from a fan of the show and not intended to lay claim to the brilliant creations of the comic or TV show on which it comments.

The Walking Dead is a modern masterpiece that feeds off (excuse the pun) a fear that has haunted human beings probably as long as we've been around: what if the dead rose and walked among us?! Well, my question is 'what if the dead rose like dough... and jam and sweet, gooey horror abounded?' That is the joke at the heart of *The Walking Bread* and I hope it's one that fans of the show as well as those who just like a delicious scare will enjoy.

Bon Appetit! And remember: 'Bite the bread and fear the filling!'

Rick Grains

May 2016

WITH THANKS TO...

ANNA VALENTINE-GROANS

EMMA SMITH-WALKER

GNAAAAAAAAARGH McGINLAY

AND ALL THE UN-DEAD TEAM AT
TRAPEZE

ABOUT
THE AUTHOR

Rick Grains awoke from a coma
to find himself in a world where the
dead had risen like dough and the
streets ran red with jam.

Joining a rag-tag group of
survivors – including a man
whose severed arm had been
replaced with a cake slice – Rick
took on the hordes of walkers,
each more delicious than the last.

He lives with his son, Coral,
somewhere in Georgia.